Colin's Correspondence

Humorous Letters to Companies & Institutions

Colin's Correspondence

© Phil Elson 2018 phil.elson1@gmail.com

Published by Phil Elson
First CreateSpace Edition 2018

A catalogue record of this book is available from the British Library.

Interior and cover design: Cassia Friello
Illustrations: Gary Standing
Illustrations: Cassia Friello / pixabay.com

To my amazing family, for all their love and support – Olga, William, Mum and Dad. I feel very blessed to have you in my life.

———

If you had to put up with three hours of commuting to an office in London every day, taking three trains each way, facing constant delays, platform changes, overcrowding, the cold and rain, all the miserable faces, what would you do to relax? What would you do for a tiny little bit of escapism?...

Table of Contents

My name is Colin Montague. Welcome to my book. I'm happily married, recently retired and I live in a charming semi-detached house in the beautiful little town of Reigate in Surrey.

Being a deep-thinker by nature, I'm always curious about the world and looking to see how it can be improved upon. From time to time I'll come up with some startlingly good ideas that are just too good to keep to myself. At the same time, I'm happy to ask for help when I need it – and you'll see some examples of that as you read through my letters. If this process has taught me anything that I could pass onto you it would be:

· Always challenge the status quo.

· Help other people when you can.

· And don't be afraid to ask for help yourself.

Anyway, I hope you enjoy reading this book and gaining a little insight into my life.

All the very best,

Colin Montague

Colin Montague, BSc (Hons), MSc

Ps. Looking back on the letters I've written over the past year it's become abundantly clear to me that, perhaps on a subconscious level, all along I've been writing a review or critique of the levels of customer service in our country. Certainly that's what my lawyer tells me I've been doing, as it allows me to publish the response letters I've received without infringing on UK copyright law!

Chapter One:
Helpful Suggestions

Even though I say so myself, I have a lot of GREAT ideas. But sometimes others are just too short-sighted to take them onboard...

For years people have bemoaned the fact that there is no word in the English language that rhymes with "orange"

Just how does the Cambridge University Press determine what to put in its Cambridge Dictionary?

5th November 2017

Dear Sir/Madam,

I sincerely hope that you will be as excited as I am to hear my news: For years people have bemoaned the fact that there is no word in the English language that rhymes with "orange". That problem is now officially over - because I have invented one. The word is "borange" and it means "A fruit or vegetable that is particularly orangey in colour, such as a cantaloupe, pumpkin, or orange". Please can you confirm by return letter that you will be including it in the next version of your most excellent dictionary.

Kind regards,
Colin Montague, BSc (Hons), MSc

17th November 2017

Dear Mr. Montague,

Thank you for your letter regarding the submission of the new word "borange". We are adding new words to the online Cambridge Dictionary all the time, but I'm afraid that we do not add words newly invented by our users. We use a number of criteria for deciding which words to include, the most important of which involves evidence of widespread, current use of a term. Please note that our dictionaries are written for learners of English, not native speakers; they are designed to help users understand English as it is currently used. They are compiled by analysing a large corpus of English texts (over 1 billion words in total) taken from all areas of writing and publishing, which allows us to see exactly how language is used.

For future reference, please note that we cannot accept suggestions for new words by letter or email. The best way for us to know that a word is missing is if you enter it in our search field and do not get a result, as we monitor searches all the time.

We hope you continue to enjoy using the online Cambridge Dictionary.

Yours sincerely,
Helen F., Commissioning Editor

Cambridge University Press

22nd November 2017

Dear Helen,

Firstly, thank you very much for taking the time to respond to my enquiry on adding the word "borange" to your dictionary. I'm naturally disappointed that you don't want to use it, and if it's okay, I would like to put forth my case:

You said you are "adding new words... all the time" and that you have to review over a billion words. So what harm is there in adding one more little one? Think of all the free publicity it could generate - it could really "put Cambridge University on the map".

As for your main criteria for accepting a word being that it's widely used, I notice you don't seem to have that problem with including "petrichor", "schwa" and "ultacrepidarian". Let's be honest here, they're about as widely used as "borange". In fact, I wouldn't be at all surprised if the person sitting nearest you at work hadn't even heard of them.

Helen, lastly, if I could provide you with concrete evidence that a few of my friends are using "borange" in regular conversation, please would you reconsider your position? Thank you again for giving this your consideration. (I'm sorry to be so forthright, but I'm genuinely passionate about the word "borange").

Kind regards,
Colin Montague, BSc (Hons), MSc

ADMIRABLE
WELL DONE C.U.P. FOR TAKING THE TIME TO GIVE A DETAILED RESPONSE!
ADMIRABLE

"Quit While You're Ahead." - A Gift to the Nation By Colin Montague

Will Tate Modern recognise a masterpiece when they see it?

17th October 2017

Dear Mr. Farquharson,

I wish to bequeath a gift to the nation, by donating to your gallery a piece of my own original artwork. To that end, I attach a photograph of the work, entitled *"Quit While You're Ahead"*.

It's dimensions are 30cm x 25cm and I painted it using water colour and acrylic paint on canvas (which I got from a branch of Tiger on Oxford Street for a bargain £3.00).

I am not prone to giving away my precious creations, but I find myself moved to do so with this particular work. Please write back at your earliest convenience to confirm your acceptance and arrange delivery.

Kind regards,
Colin Montague,
BSc (Hons), MSc

19th February 2017

Dear Colin,

Thank you for your letter of 17 October 2017 and your generous offer to donate your work *Quit While You're Ahead* to Tate Modern.

Regrettably, after due consideration, it has been decided that we are unable to accept your kind offer. As I am sure you understand, we must consider all works offered within Tate's overall acquisitions strategy, and also take into account the increasing pressures on our budgets and resources related to the care, storage and display of works. Unfortunately, we frequently find ourselves forced to decline offers of gifts to the collection.

I am sorry not to be able to send you a more positive reply, but would like to thank you for your generosity towards Tate.

Yours sincerely,
Ares., Administrator Collections & Curator

Curatorial Department
Tate Modern

25th February 2017

Dear Ares,

Thank you very much for your letter. I completely understand your point – the costs associated with storage and display can be very expensive. So how about if I make a *much smaller* version?

Would that help drive down the costs?

Kind regards,
Colin Montague, BSc (Hons), MSc

the softer scooper for your pooper

Is Kimberley-Clark willing to consider an idea for a new advertising slogan?

28th September 2017

Dear Sir/Madam,

I am a loyal customer of your Andrex toilet paper (especially the shea butter variety, which I find particularly gentle and forgiving). I recently saw your advert, which stated "Be kind on your behind" and it made me smile. It actually inspired me to think of a few alternatives you might want to use. For example: "Andrex....

- take the smear off your rear"

- wipe the dump off your rump"

- clean the cack out your crack"

- clear what reeks off your cheeks"

- the softer scooper for your pooper"

I would be delighted if you wanted to use one of these for future advertising campaigns. So please let me know what you think and whether you are at all interested in using one. I hope to hear from you soon with your thoughts.

Kind regards,
Colin Montague, BSc (Hons), MSc

5th October 2017

Dear Mr. Montague,

Thank you for your recent letter regarding ANDREX® toilet tissue.

While we appreciate your taking the time to share your thoughts, we are not permitted to accept suggestions from the public for the advertising or promotion of our products. This would include any suggestions relating to the fields of artwork or product display, suggested slogans, product names or trademarks. Since we have our own advertising team and work with specific advertising agencies, we have this policy to prevent misunderstandings as to the origin of an idea. Over the years, it has proved to be in the best interest of all concerned.

Thank you again for your interest in Kimberly-Clark Corporation. We appreciate the time you have taken to contact us.

Yours sincerely,
Pietro M., Consumer Services Department

Kimberley-Clark

MARVELLOUS! K.C WERE CERTAINLY VERY POLITE!

How open-mined is Canterbury City Council to change?

28th September 2017

Dear Sir/Madam,

Firstly, let me say I love visiting your beautiful city - particularly the awe-inspiring cathedral. I'm actually writing to offer a suggestion, which before you dismiss it out of hand, I'd urge you to give it some serious thought: I think you should change the name of the town from Canterbury to *Can*-erbury. It has a better ring to it and gives a much more positive message.

I've asked my wife and she agrees, so I really think there's something to this. Also, I imagine it would earn the town a lot of free publicity and attract many more tourists.

Please let me know your thoughts, as I am keen to see if you think this idea has any merit.

Kind regards,
Colin Montague, BSc (Hons), MSc

1st November 2017

Dear Mr. Montague,

Thank you for your letter and my apologies for the delayed reply.

It is always lovely to hear that people enjoy visiting Canterbury. I agree that it is a beautiful city and has so much to offer. You may be interested to hear that we've just heard that the city has once again received Gold at the recent Britain in Bloom awards. Another testament to our great city.

I have looked at your suggestion regarding the change of name and discussed it with the Chief Executive here. While the sentiment behind the idea is great, and I have no doubt it would generate a huge amount of publicity, I'm sure you will understand that the name itself is steeped in history. As the home of the Mother Church of the worldwide Anglican faith and the seat of the Archbishop of Canterbury a name change would need significant backing from a wide range of stakeholders and so would not be in the gift of the city council alone.

However, we will continue to work hard to improve and take pride in our city. Welcoming visitors is a key part of our local economy and we hope that you will enjoy visiting for many years to come.

Thank you for taking the time to write.

Kind regards
Caroline H., Head of Business & Regeneration

Canterbury City Council

BRILLIANT
AND IT SOUNDS AS IF I WAS SO CLOSE TO MAKING IT HAPPEN!
ANSWER!

I want to do my bit to help the environment, so I have an idea for you to consider...

LOVELY PEOPLE! LOVELY COFFEE!

My edible coffee cup: saving the planet – one sip at a time!

This topic really hit the headlines in 2018 (possibly thanks to this letter?). Caffè Nero is trying to do the right thing.

27th January 2017

Dear Sir/Madam,

I'm a huge fan of Caffè Nero and I buy your take-away coffees all the time. In fact I can sometimes get through five large lattes in one day (sugar-free syrup - I'm on a diet). Anyway, I'm not just writing to tell you how much I love your coffee, but also how much I admire your ethical approach to business, as outlined on your excellent website.

It made me think I want to do my bit to help the environment, so I have an idea for you to consider – edible coffee cups! If you think about it, it's so simple, it's genius! As you drink the coffee you eat the cup... result: NO WASTE. I've recently been experimenting at home with biscuit cups, but unfortunately they just go all soggy and break. As for my milk chocolate cup experiment, the less said the better – I'm still cleaning out the carpet stains!

But I really think I'm onto something big here. So it would be absolutely amazing if you wanted to take my idea forward and make it a reality. Cutting down on waste is vital for our planet, so I look forward to hearing your thoughts on this important idea to help the environment.

Kind regards,
Colin Montague, BSc (Hons), MSc

7th February 2017

Dear Mr. Montague,

Thank you for taking the time to write to us here at Caffè Nero regarding your idea of edible coffee cups.

I have forwarded your comments to the Head of Supply here and I am sure he will be in touch should we choose to investigate the possibility of edible cups in the future.

Once again thank you very much for sharing your ideas with us. We wish you the best of luck in the future.

Kind Regards,
Tracey T., Customer Services

Caffè Nero Group Ltd

I think I've stumbled across a brilliant idea that could really be a game-changer...

Is the popular confectioner, Cadbury, willing to consider my radically new concept?

26th January 2017

Dear Sir/Madam,

Firstly, let me say I've always been a big fan of Cadbury's products. But I'm sure that, like me, you share my concern about the growing epidemic of child obesity sweeping across our country. I only have to look at some of the "chunky" kids getting on my bus each morning to know it's a major problem in modern society (last week, one boy was so out of breath standing, I actually had to give up my seat for him).

To that end, I think I've stumbled across a brilliant idea that could really be a game-changer in the fight for our children's health...

Cadbury makes "Dairy Milk" chocolate bars. And as we know from your advertising over the years, each one contains "a glass and a half of milk". Well then, what if you took some of that milk and starting bottling and selling it separately? If you think about it, you could still market it as "Dairy Milk" (because that's what it would be - literally) – you wouldn't even have to change the branding.

Suddenly, children are healthier, parents are happier and your profits go up - surely that's a win-win? I'm genuinely excited by this idea, so I would very much like to know if you think it has any merit.

Kind regards,
Colin Montague, BSc (Hons), MSc

6th March 2017

Dear Mr. Montague,

Thank you for sharing your idea with us. It's an interesting one and we have already explored a number of ideas very similar to yours.

Our marketing and development teams are always working on new products so it is quite possible that the idea you suggested may be one which the company is already working on. Whenever we bring out a new product it's the result of a tremendous amount of time and money. For every new product that makes it onto the shelves, many fall by the wayside for one reason or another. We have to be sure that every new product has mass appeal, so we base our decisions on extensive market research.

We receive a large number of suggestions from consumers and entrepreneurs, but in order to avoid misunderstandings over ownership of rights, we are unable to accept any ideas from outside the company's specialist development teams and agencies. Whilst we won't be using your idea at this time we would like to thank you again for sharing it with us and for your interest in our brands and products. If there's anything else we can do for you, please do not hesitate to contact us again.

Yours Sincerely,
Joana, Consumer Conversations Consultant

Mondelez International

EXCELLENT I'M A BIG FAN OF CADBURY! RESPONSE

Many branches of Starbucks are so popular it can sometimes be hard to get a seat. Thankfully, I have a solution.

28th January 2017

Dear Sir/Madam,

I am a regular visitor to several Starbucks branches in London and Southeast England. I'm writing to you to express a concern and offer a potential solution. Namely, when I buy my usual grande, decaf, sugar-free hazelnut, skinny, no foam, extra-hot latte, I then look for a seat and can never get one.

There's always some young bearded man with a laptop sitting there for two hours, taking up four sofa seats, face buried in his computer and nursing a quarter inch of coffee at the bottom of his cup. Or groups of mothers, who seem to have finished their drinks long ago, obliviously chatting away to each other. It's really not fair on others - and it must reduce the flow of customers (thus eating into your profits).

So I propose a wristband system, whereby when you get your coffee you're given a coloured band. After half an hour a barista simply calls out "red bands out" (like they used to in public swimming pools). Alternatively, you could give each customer a hand-held buzzer, like they have in some restaurants in the US when people are waiting for a table) which could "go off" at a set time – then they've got to go!

I would be very grateful to know your thoughts on my idea, as it's certainly more practical than my initial one of just banning certain groups from sitting down.

Kind regards,
Colin Montague, BSc (Hons), MSc

I buy my usual grande, decaf, sugar-free hazelnut, skinny, no foam, extra-hot latte

1st February 2017

Dear Colin,

Thank you for taking the time to contact Starbucks Coffee Company.

Customer feedback is a critical measure of our success in providing you with quality products and excellent service. I therefore appreciate your feedback and would like to assure you that your comments have been shared with the appropriate people for their attention.

Thank you again for taking the time to share your thoughts with us and for giving us the opportunity to improve our operations.

I hope you will continue enjoying our coffee for many years to come.

Yours sincerely,
Gina S., Customer Care Specialist

Starbucks Coffee Compay (UK) Limited

TOP-NOTCH! STILL LOVING THEIR LATTES!

Collin

I have a new idea, which I'm hoping the Conservative Party will adopt as official policy...

Conservative Campaign Headquarters was the only major party that responded to my great idea.

12th November 2017

Dear Sir/Madam,

I have a new idea, which I'm hoping the Conservative Party will adopt as official policy, as I truly believe it will win votes and be very good for the country: As Britain goes through the economic challenges brought on by the uncertainty of Brexit, we need simple and effective ways to become more competitive as a nation. So I would introduce laws to drastically limit the number of toilet breaks taken on company time.

Let's say hypothetically each employee goes to the toilet for a total of around 12 minutes per workday, while at work, but outside of lunch and tea breaks. If we said there were 40 million workers each working 240 days a year – that's a staggering 1.92 billion hours per year that are lost on company-time toilet breaks. Even if we said the average lost productivity of those 12 minutes was as low as £20, that's £38.4 billion lost to the national economy that we could claim back.

I'm very excited about my idea. Please can you let me know your thoughts.

Kind regards,
Colin Montague, BSc (Hons), MSc

30th November 2017

Dear Mr. Montague,

Thank you for taking the time to write to the Conservative Party with your suggestion on increasing the nation's competitiveness.

It was certainly an interesting idea and one you have clearly put a lot of thought into, arriving at the calculations you have. Whilst I am not certain that this is an area the Government is able to bring in legislation I will be sure to pass your suggestion on.

Thank you again for taking the time to get in contact.

Kind regards,
Kayli F., Chairman's Correspondence Secretary

Conservative Campaign Headquarters

TERRIFIC! CONGRATULATIONS ON BEING THE ONLY PARTY THAT RESPONDED! TERRIFIC!

What if you simply changed the timetable?

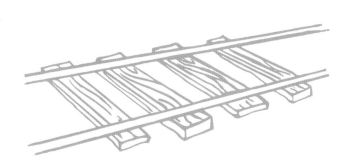

Will Govia Thameslink Railway take on my revolutionary concept?

20th November 2017

Dear Sir/Madam,

I very occasionally take the approximately one-hour journey up to London on the Reigate train and am aware of all the disruption caused by industrial action over the past couple of years. Regarding this, I have a suggestion on which I would value your opinion:

A friend who makes a similar journey every day told me she and many others have received quite a lot of refund money for trains that were delayed more than 30 minutes. But it seems ludicrous to me that strike action is causing you to lose all your revenue – if you don't make money, people will end up losing their jobs.

So I am writing because an idea struck me: What if you simply changed the timetable to state that Reigate to London takes three hours? That way, there are no refunds and if the trains arrive any quicker, it would be a pleasant surprise. It seems like such a simple solution.

I hope you find this helpful and I would be most grateful if you could give me your opinion as to the workability of the idea.

King regards,
Colin Montague, BSc (Hons), MSc

27th November 2017

Dear Mr. Montague,

Thank you for contacting us with regards to your idea to help improve our performance.

We appreciated all feedback and suggestions, good or bad, and therefore I have logged down the suggestion you have provided. All logs are reviewed by senior managers for possible talking points in their upcoming meetings, it may be that yours may be one of those although I cannot promise it will.

Thank you once again for writing in with your idea and I hope that your future journeys with us will be pleasant.

Yours sincerely,
Katherine G., Contact Centre Manager

Southern Rail Customer Services

SUPERB!

I'VE STILL GOT MY FINGERS CROSSED THAT THEY'LL ADOPT MY SUGGESTION!

SUPERB!

I'm very excited to tell you about my idea for an advert you could put on television next February...

I imagine Poundland are still considering my idea.

21st April 2017

Dear Sir,

I'm very excited to tell you about my idea for an advert you could put on television next February. Here it is... We start with a close-up of one of your plastic bags full of shopping. Soul music plays in the background.

The camera slowly pans back to reveal it's sitting in front of a closed bedroom door. A gentle rhythmic slapping sound builds up, like a man with sweaty hands clapping - but wetter. Some low male and female moans are introduced.

Then finally a seductive female voice purrs "For the sexiest discount shopping this Valentine's Day......................take your partner to Poundland!"

I think because it's only suggestive, it keeps everything quite classy. I assume you agree. Please write back to me at your earliest convenience, so we can discuss my payment.

Kind regards,
Colin Montague, BSc (Hons), MSc

WONDERFUL COMPANY!
I THINK FOR LOTS OF PEOPLE POUNDLAND IS THEIR FAVOURITE SHOP!

STILL AWAITING A RESPONSE

It always seems to rain a lot in Reigate...

GREAT!

FOR ME, SURREY IS DEFINITELY THE COUNTRY'S NO.1 COUNTY

GREAT!

I expect Surrey County Council is still conducting studies to prove my theory before leaping into action.

16th February 2017

Dear Sir/Madam,

I am a Surrey resident and also something of an amateur meteorologist. I am writing to make a suggestion which I feel will greatly benefit the town of Reigate.

It always seems to rain a lot in Reigate. More so than most other towns. When I ask friends if they agree if it rains more in Reigate they almost always say "Yes, it does". Now on the North side of town is Reigate Hill. Coincidence? I think not! The gulf-stream is obviously crossing the Atlantic, picking up moisture, getting as far as Reigate Hill and dumping rain on the town below. Result - misery.

My solution is common sense: simply remove the top of Reigate Hill. The heavy air won't have to lose water to get over it and then it will rain on London instead. There's hardly any housing on that hill, so the impact would be absolutely negligible. The earth removed could easily be put in the dry moat in the nearby Castle Grounds, just behind the high street.

I would greatly appreciate hearing from you as to whether this idea has any merit. Personally, I believe it could really boost tourism in the area and put Reigate on the map.

Best regards,
Colin Montague, BSc (Hons), MSc

STILL AWAITING A RESPONSE

Chapter Two:
Simple Requests

I tend to find that most people in life are incredibly kind and helpful, even when confronted with something they're not expecting. Of course, that's not always the case...

As you can imagine, I rarely go out to dinner, but this is a special occasion

---

What will The Clock House Restaurant make of my request to enjoy their fine dining?

27th January 2017

Dear Sir/Madam,

My wife and I are celebrating our 25th wedding anniversary next month and we would like to enjoy a memorable experience in a great restaurant.

Unfortunately, I need to discuss a rather delicate matter with you in advance of our booking. For the past few years I have suffered from fairly extreme flatulence. Sometimes it's controllable, but at other times I can't hold back. I have tried a variety of different diets, but nothing seems to really improve the situation.

As you can imagine, I rarely go out to dinner, but this is a special occasion. I was wondering whether you perhaps had a private dining area we could use. If not, could you seat us in a corner by an open window or door? I can usually avoid making a sound, but it might also be useful if you could put us in a noisier section of the restaurant – perhaps near the kitchens or under a loud speaker, if you play music.

Thanks in advance for your discretion in dealing with this matter. Please could you let me know what, if any, arrangements you can make. I look forward to hearing from you at your earliest convenience.

Kind regards,
Colin Montague, BSc (Hons), MSc

31st January 2017

Dear Mr. Montague,

Thank you for your letter of 27th January concerning your 25th wedding anniversary celebration and your rather delicate matter.

We are delighted that you wish to celebrate your 25th wedding anniversary at The Clock House Restaurant and I believe the best solution would be for you and Mrs. Montague to dine in our alcove which is a semi-private area. This does depend, however, on whether we have a large table in for dinner that evening as we seat tables of six and above in the alcove. We are generally fully booked on Saturday evenings so I do hope that you would be able to dine with us on a week day.

Perhaps you would be kind enough to call our Receptionist on 01483 ****** who will be delighted to make the reservation for you, if our alcove is free the evening you wish to dine with us. We would note that it is a 25th wedding anniversary celebration so that we mark this very special occasion.

Yours sincerely,
Serina D., Managing Director

The Clock House

WORLD-CLASS! THAT IS GENUINELY FIRST-RATE SERVICE!

Beaverbrook is an excellent fine-dining restaurant – but how will it react when confronted with a difficult moral dilemma?

28th September 2017

Dear Sir/Madam,

I'm writing to you with an unusual request. I'm quite embarrassed to ask, but I've got myself into a bit of a pickle: A few months ago I went to the States on holiday and there I met a charming couple, Bob and Lindy, from Wyoming. We became friends and now they are planning to go to dinner with me when they visit London in early November.

The problem is that when we first met I got a bit carried away with things and told them I was the Duke of Crawley. Now it's too late for me to back out of it. I've been very silly, but it would be extremely awkward to have to explain to them at this stage and I'm worried it would end our friendship and spoil their trip.

So I was wondering if I could perhaps book a table at your restaurant under the name "The Duke of Crawley" and ask your waiting staff to refer to me either as either "Sir" or "Your Grace", maybe even with a slight bow. I would certainly be willing to pay a little extra on the bill for your inconvenience (£20?, £40? - just let me know what would be appropriate).

As soon as you confirm that you can accommodate my request I will immediately make the reservation. I'm rather anxious about the whole issue, so I hope to hear from you at your earliest convenience.

Kind regards,
Colin Montague, BSc (Hons), MSc

A few months ago I went to the States on holiday and there I met a charming couple, Bob and Lindy, from Wyoming...

4th October 2017

Dear Mr. Montague,

Thank you for your letter but unfortunately, we are unable to accommodate your request.

Kind regards,
Suzie W.

Beaverbrook

MAGNIFICENT! ABSOLUTELY RIGHT. CLEARLY OPERATING TO THE HIGHEST MORAL PRINCIPLES!

to be frank, I'm writing because I have an embarrassing problem...

What will the Boringdon Hall Hotel make of this? It's one thing to have a problem; it's another to type it on paper.

26th January 2017

Dear Sir/Madam,

I'm planning on visiting my younger sister in late July this year and I'm considering staying at your hotel, because I know that the Boringdon Hall Hotel has a great reputation for looking after it's guests. To be frank, I'm writing because I have an embarrassing problem, suffering from a reasonably mild form of Tourette's Syndrome.

As I'm sure you're aware, it means that quite often I can't stop myself from shouting out a random word. I don't want to annoy any other guests, so I carrot wanted to find out if it would be possible to book a room in a separate area POTATO! or perhaps at the end of a corridor.

Thankfully, I'm often able to control myself enough to substitute swear words, but it can still be pretty uncomfortable for people within earshot.

I look forward to bum, BUM! (sorry, this is my last sheet of typing paper) hearing from you at your earliest convenience, at which time I can hopefully book my five-night stay.

Kind regards,
Colin Montague, BSc (Hons), MSc

30th January 2017

Dear Mr. Monatgue,

Thank you for your letter that we have received regarding you wishing to come and stay with us.

We would of course be delighted to welcome you to Boringdon Hall & Gaia Spa.

In regards to booking a separate room away from other guests, we would be more than happy to do this for you if you wished. However we do not feel this will be necessary regardless of your Tourette's syndrome. I am sure will have a room suitable for you through the hotel and please do not feel for one minute that you would make any of our other guests uncomfortable.

Do you have any particular dates or type of room in mind that you are looking for, we will happily check the availability for you and find the best package to suit you. We have The Royal suite, The Executive suite, Four Poster suites and our Courtyard rooms within the hotel depending on availability we can see what we can put together for you.

It would be a real pleasure for both myself and the team for you to come and stay with us to enjoy everything we have to offer. Please do not hesitate to contact me personally or our reservations team if you would like any further information.

I look forward to speaking with and hopefully meeting you in person, very soon.

Kindest Regards
Amber E.,
Front of House Manager

Boringdon Hall Hotel

JUST...
EVERYONE SHOULD WANT TO STAY WITH SUCH COMMENABLE PEOPLE!
EXCEPTIONAL!

I want to assure you that I would always enter and leave the hotel in normal everyday clothes and I would not soil the linen.

How open-minded is the management at the popular Drakes Hotel?

13th March 2017

Dear Sir/Madam,

My wife and I would like to book a few weekday nights in July at your hotel to celebrate our 25th wedding anniversary, because we've heard great things about how you go out of your way to look after your guests. I'm writing because I have a rather sensitive matter I wanted to run past you first to make sure we're all comfortable before we proceed with the booking.

Over the years I have come to realise that I am an autonepiophiliac – in layman's terms, I have adult baby syndrome (ABS), whereby I generally feel more relaxed and comfortable in a state of regressive role play as a baby. This includes drinking from a baby bottle, wearing a nappy and crawling on the floor.

I want to assure you that I would always enter and leave the hotel in normal everyday clothes and I would not soil the linen. It's just that we tend to order room service when we're away and I don't want to give anyone a fright if they see me in my nappy with a dummy in my mouth and baby bonnet.

Please could you confirm whether this will be okay by return letter, and assuming I receive a positive response I will go ahead and make our booking.

Best regards,
Colin Montague, BSc (Hons), MSc

17th March 2017

Dear Mr. Montague,

Thank you for your letter explaining the circumstances of your booking.

We are more than happy for you to book with us and do not see any problem with staff members attending to your room service.

We must stipulate that this would be in your room only, which I think you mentioned in your letter.

If you would like to book a room at Drakes, please call on 01273 ****** or book via our website at www.drakesofbrighton.com

We look forward to hearing from you.

Kindest regards
J Underhill

Drakes Hotel

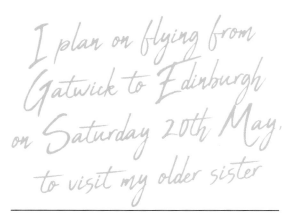

I plan on flying from Gatwick to Edinburgh on Saturday 20th May, to visit my older sister

Can the well-respected airline, Flybe, accept a rather unusual passenger?

17th January 2017

Dear Sir/Madam,

I plan on flying from Gatwick to Edinburgh on Saturday 20th May, to visit my older sister. I would like to bring Derek with me - my emotional support animal. He is a miniature pig.

I have only had Derek a short time, but we have already developed a close bond. As a nervous flyer, I feel that being with him will greatly reduce my anxiety during the trip. He really is quite tiny and will just sit quietly on my lap, perhaps letting out the occasional low "oink". Then afterwards I will simply pop him in my satchel and get on our way.

I'm writing because I would like to ask a small favour - if I confirm in writing which flights I've booked, please could you ensure that on these flights the attendants do not offer us any ham sandwiches, pork scratchings, bacon crisps, etc. - I don't mind them being served to others, but I really don't want to hurt Derek's feelings (we don't need both of us feeling anxious).

As soon as you can confirm this, I will book the flights and advise you of the dates. I look forward to hearing from you in the near future.

Kind regards,
Colin Montague, BSc (Hons), MSc

25th January 2017

Dear Colin,

Thank you for contacting us regarding your intended travel plans and Derek, your emotional support animal.

While I appreciate your requirement for the emotional support provided by Derek, I must inform you that we cannot carry Derek in the cabin on our flights. He will be unable to travel on your lap or within a small satchel. If you require Derek as an ESA in Edinburgh, it may be possible to arrange for Derek to travel safely within the hold of the aircraft. I appreciate that Derek will not be able to provide the same level of emotional support for your flight from this position, though we will not be able to accommodate him otherwise.

To arrange for Derek to travel in the hold of the aircraft, please contact our cargo team directly on 01332 ******.

Flybe will always endeavor to meet needs of our passengers and I regret that we cannot permit Derek to travel with you in-flight. If there is other assistance we can provide to make your flight more comfortable, such as assistance through the airport or to your seat, please write back to us or email us at 'specialassistance@flybe.com'.

Should your experience be negatively impacted by the offer of pork, bacon or ham on board, please let us know your Flybe booking reference number once you have booked. We will ask our crew to avoid offering you these products. You can also mention this to any of our team at the time of boarding and they will similarly withhold pork-related products.

We like to make our flights as comfortable and welcoming as possible, and I hope that you will still be able to take advantage of our services in the future.

Kind regards,
Sam B., Social Media Agent

Flybe

He is really quite tiny and will just sit quietly on my lap, perhaps letting out the occasional low "oink"

oink

oink

Will National Express accept my travelling companion?

1st February 2017

Dear Sir/Madam,

I was originally wanting to fly from Gatwick to Edinburgh on Saturday 20th May to visit my sister. But my plans now need to be changed, because I have learnt that I will not be permitted to fly with Derek, my emotional support animal. As a result, I am now strongly considering travelling by National Express coach from London Victoria instead.

Derek is a miniature pig and although we have only been together a few months, in that time we have definitely built up a strong attachment to each other. As a rather nervous traveller, I know that being with him is therapeutic and will greatly reduce my anxiety during the long trip. He really is just a little chap, and he'll almost certainly just sit calmly on my lap, grunting softly to himself.

Please can you confirm that Derek will be welcome on your coach and then I can book my tickets. Also, I have a small favour to ask – can we be assured a window seat, as I'm sure Derek will want to look out of the window.

Thank you in advance for your assistance. I look forward to hearing from you in the near future.

Kind regards,
Colin Montague, BSc (Hons), MSc

7th February 2017

Dear Colin,

Thank you for taking the time in contacting us.

Your request has been passed on to our Safety Department who will advise us of our full policy and any risks of taking the assistance pet you have.

We will be in contact shortly with our findings to advise if travel can be allowed or not.

Thank you again for taking the time to contact us, your feedback is greatly appreciated. If we may be of any further assistance please do not hesitate to contact us on 03717 ******; our lines are available between the hours of 08:00 and 22:00.

Yours Sincerely,
Akhtar H., Executive Complaints Colleague

National Express

12th March 2017

Dear Mr. Hussain,

Thank you for your letter dated 7th February in response to my question regarding taking Derek, my emotional support animal, with me to Scotland. It's been while and I was wondering if your Safety Department has now had a chance to review his case. Just to take issue on one minor point – he's not strictly a "pet", he's an emotional support animal – so even though we are very close, in effect I consider him to be a working pig (like a guide pig for the blind).

Please can you advise if I can travel with him on your coaches as soon as possible, as I am anxious to book up my tickets to visit my sister.

Thank you again for your understanding and assistance.

Kind regards,
Colin Montague, BSc (Hons), MSc

14th March 2017

Dear Colin,

Thank you for your letter, please accept my apologies for the delay in responding to your request. I have sought advice and require the following so we can consider your request further.

1. A copy of your APHA license and CPH number.

2. Confirmation from your GP to confirm the need to travel with a pig for medical reasons.

As soon as we are in receipt of these I will contact you again. It would be nice to talk to you personally so could you supply a telephone number please. Alternatively you can contact me on the number below.

I look forward to hearing from you soon.

Yours Sincerely
Claire H., Customer Service Manager

National Express

20th March 2017

Dear Claire,

Thank you for your prompt reply. Unfortunately, I have just discovered some rather disturbing news – it transpires that Derek isn't a miniature pig after all - he's just a normal pig. I have been mis-sold a supposedly miniature pig!

I first had my suspicions when I noticed he was beginning to grow at an almost exponential rate. In fact, I now calculate that by the time I travel to see my sister in Scotland, Derek will be six months old and weigh in excess of 250 lbs. I'm guessing that's probably too big to fit into your coach – even if I buy him an extra seat (please confirm).

To make matters worse, I'm getting the distinct impression that Derek is also a nervous passenger, like me. So now I'm considering getting him his own emotional support animal, so he can feel mentally strong enough to give me the emotional support I need. I'm torn between getting him a badger or an otter – what do you think would be more practical?

Any suggestions you can provide would be greatly appreciated.

Kind regards,
Colin Montague, BSc (Hons), MSc

Here's some more of my artwork:
Taking Derek for a walk
on Reigate Hill

(But the Tate's
not having these
two gems!)

Would that be distracting or upsetting for any of the animals?

I'm a big fan of Edinburgh Zoo's giant panda.

9th November 2017

Dear Sir/Madam,

My wife and I are planning a trip to Edinburgh in February, as we hope to see the Scotland vs. England rugby match. I am writing because we also plan on visiting your zoo, primarily because we are huge fans of giant pandas and we would like to see your beautiful Yang Guang (in fact we have just returned from a trip to Hong Kong, where we saw the amazing Ying Ying in the Asian animal centre at Ocean Park).

More specifically, if we pay for a zookeeper experience, will we be able to meet Yang Guang? As a follow up question (and this may sound a little odd…) would we be able to wear our panda onesies for the day – or would that be distracting or upsetting for any of the animals?

I appreciate this might be an unusual request, so that is why I have taken the trouble to write to you in advance. Please could you let me know your response by return letter.

Kind regards,
Colin Montague, BSc (Hons), MSc

19th November 2017

Dear Colin,

Thank you for your letter enquiring about the Giant Pandas.

I'm afraid it isn't possible for us to offer an up-close experience with our Giant Pandas. Our pandas are wild animals that have been raised without prolonged human contact and tend to react badly when approached by strangers. As well as this they are very territorial and have been shown to experience heightened levels of stress when people enter their territory.

In regards to the panda onesies, unfortunately we wouldn't be able to allow this as it can upset some of the animals.

In February visits to the pandas are non-ticketed and therefore you can visit the enclosure any time between 10.30 and 15.30.

In February we will have our Giant Lanterns of China Festival in full swing. If you have time before or after the rugby I would recommend trying to come along. They are in the process of setting up some of the lanterns now and they look incredible. Details of the lantern festival can be found online but I have also inserted a leaflet for you to have a look at.

I hope you have a great time in Edinburgh and enjoy your visit to Edinburgh Zoo as well as your trip to the rugby.

Kind regards,
Hannah, Admissions and Retail Assistant

Edinburgh Zoo

22nd November 2017

Dear Hannah,

Thank you very much indeed for taking the time to respond to my letter – it was very kind of you. We have now booked our travel and hotel and we are really looking forward to seeing your panda enclosure when we visit the zoo, albeit from behind the barrier like everyone else!

Just to clarify one point you mentioned - is it specifically the panda onesies that would be a problem, or would any animal-style onesies still upset the animals? (e.g. piglet or dragon costumes). I'm assuming it's not onesies in general (e.g. super hero onesies).

We do have other clothing options, so this shouldn't be a problem, but I would still like to know.

Kind regards,
Colin Montague, BSc (Hons), MSc

1st December 2017

Dear Colin,

Thank you for your letter!

As a follow up to the previous letter I'm afraid we do not allow any onesies into Edinburgh Zoo, as stated in our terms and conditions on our website, to respect animal welfare. Visitors may be asked to remove any onesies before entering the park. Please follow this link to our terms and conditions for more information on this: http://www.edinburghzoo. org.uk/plan-your-visit/dayplanner/edinburgh-zoo-entry-terms-and-conditions/

Kind regards,
Mhairi, Admissions and Retail Team

Edinburgh Zoo

DISTINGUISHED! EVERYBODY SHOULD VISIT THIS ZOO!

Before I make a booking...

The Balmoral Hotel in Edinburgh is clearly a great hotel for humans, but what about for pigs?

25th November 2017

Dear Sir/Madam,

I plan on driving up to Edinburgh next April to visit my sister and I am writing well in advance, because I have a particular issue I need to discuss: I am a particularly nervous traveller, so I benefit greatly from being accompanied by Jemima, my new emotional support pig. She is a clean and very well-behaved miniature pig and we now go everywhere together. She really is no trouble at all and she will always be properly bathed and dressed smartly, in-keeping with a five-star hotel.

Before I make the booking (probably for a double room for 5 nights), please can you confirm that this will not be a problem. I also plan on doing some sightseeing with Jemima when I'm there, so it would be very helpful if you were able to identify any attractions I can visit with her.

Thank you very much in advance for any assistance you can provide.

Kind regards,
Colin Montague, BSc (Hons), MSC

30th November 2017

Dear Mr. Montague,

Thank you for your letter dated 25th November 2017 enquiring your potential future visit to The Balmoral Hotel. We are happy to accommodate Jemima during your visit. I would like to ask for the size of Jemima since we don't allow pets/support animals over 20 lbs. Please find attached our Pet Policy with important information with regards to Jemima's stay at the hotel. Please read carefully before making a booking. The pet policy refers only to cats and dogs but in this case also refers to Jemima. If you would decide to make a booking please contact me.

If you have any other questions or concerns please do not hesitate to contact me.

With warm regards,
Rob E., Director of Rooms

The Balmoral Edinburgh

PET POLICY

The Balmoral, Edinburgh is delighted to welcome pets. Guests are required to please sign this letter of acceptance of the policies listed below.

• Pets are restricted to dogs and cats only and must weigh less than 20 lbs unless prior written consent of the hotel's management is received.

• 1 pet maximum per room. A fee of £50 per stay, or every 15 nights, will be applied to pets (excluding Assistance Dogs). They will receive a Pet Welcome Pack consisting of a bed, water bowl, welcome treats, a list of pet friendly restaurants, bars and parks, contact details of local dog walkers.

• A cleaning fee of £250 will be applied to cover any speciality deep cleaning or damage following checkout.

• The Housekeeping Department will service the guest room when a pet is not in the room. Please contact Reception for service times.

• We ask that pets are kept on a leash while on hotel property other than when in the guestroom or suite.

• Please do not leave your pet unattended in your guest room. A list of pet-sitters is available from Reception.

• Pets are not allowed in any food and beverage outlets, Spa and Fitness area, or Pool area within the hotel. This policy does not apply to Assistance Dogs.

• Guests must always clean up after their pet on hotel property and in the neighbourhood.

• Barking must be controlled by the owner to avoid inconvenience to other guests.

• Guests are responsible for all property damages and/or personal injuries resulting from their pet. Guests agree to indemnify and hold harmless the hotel and its owners from all liability and damage suffered as a result of the guests pet.

• The hotel reserves the right to charge a guests account commensurate to the cost of such damages.

PETS NAME: *Jemima*

Accepted and agreed to on

                                         -(day, month and year)

Guest

                                           The Balmoral, Edinburgh

Colin Montague
_____

Please print name/title

                                         _____

                                           Please print name/title

5th December 2017

Dear Rob,

Thank you for your recent reply, explaining that you will allow Jemima to stay with me at your hotel - that's fantastic news! Being a young micro pig, she just fits within your 20lb maximum weight restriction. However, we must be clear on one point: Jemima is not a "pet"; as an emotional support animal, she is very much a working pig (like a rescue pig or drug detection pig).

There is only one small additional issue, which I need to clarify prior to making our booking: This weekend, I have learnt that Jemima is pregnant. I'm very happy about this, but it does present us with a logistical issue. The gestation period for her breed is only three months, three weeks and three days. This means that by the time of our travel in April we should be joined by a litter of up to ten baby piglets - all of which should thankfully fit well within your maximum weight restriction of 20lbs (so I can't imagine that would be a problem).

Given this latest development, before I make the booking for five nights, please can you confirm the additional charges. Under the circumstances, I would very much appreciate a group discount.

Kind regards,
Colin Montague, BSc (Hons), MSc

20th December 2017

Dear Mr. Montague,

Thank you for your letter and let me first congratulate you with Jemima's pregnancy. I hope Jemima will have an uneventful pregnancy and will give birth to some beautiful offspring.

Whilst I am very happy for Jemima, unfortunately we are unable to accommodate yourself, Jemima and her baby piglets in the hotel. As mentioned before, we would be happy to accommodate Jemima but we cannot make an exception for the baby piglets.

If you are able to find a babysitter or able to make other arrangements for the piglets we would be happy to offer you a competitive rate for a stay at The Balmoral.

I would like to wish you and Jemima a Merry Christmas and a Happy New Year.

With warm regards,
Rob E., Director of Rooms

The Balmoral Edinburgh

I could probably make some money if I were to get a tattoo...

Will Wrigley sponsor me getting a tattoo on my behind?

15th November 2017

Dear Sir/Madam,

I'm not sure who is the best person to talk to, but I have a serious business proposition for you to consider. For several years now I have wanted to get a tattoo (right now, I don't have any on my body). Then it struck me that I could probably make some money if I were to get a tattoo of a major corporation's name and slogan.

To this end, I would like to propose that I get a 12cm x 6cm tattoo on my left buttock that says "Skittles" and a similar - sized one on my right buttock that says "Taste the rainbow!" Please rest assured that it would be done tastefully and per your strict brand guidelines.

I think it could generate a lot of publicity for your company at a very reasonable cost. Please let me know whether or not you are interested and then we can work out a suitable level of compensation.

I look forward to receiving your response.

Kind regards,
Colin Montague, BSc (Hons), MSc

20th November 2017

Dear Mr. Montague,

Thank you for contacting us outlining an opportunity to be involved with sponsoring you.

All our sponsorships are chosen for their relevance to our business and sadly your proposal is not the best fit for the brand and does not tie in with our other planned marketing activities.

We hope you will understand our reasons for declining.

Yours sincerely,
Simon, Consumer Care Administrator

The Wrigley Company Ltd

22nd November 2017

Dear Simon,

Thank you very much for your response. I understand exactly where you are coming from. In retrospect, it seems obvious now that my suggestion of tattooing "Skittles – Taste the rainbow" on my buttocks was never going to be a good fit for this particular product.

Having given it some more thought, I think tattooing "Hubba Bubba" on my bum cheeks instead would be a far better brand marketing fit. Please could you consider this proposal and let me know if this works.

Kind regards,
Colin Montague, BSc (Hons), MSc

14th December 2017

Dear Simon Montague,

Thank you for contacting us about your WRIGLEY marketing idea.

We've a dedicated team whose job it is to research and design new products and ideas but it's always great to hear from you.

If you need any further information or advice, please don't hesitate to get in touch.

Yours sincerely,
Javeen Bentley, Consumer Care Team

The Wrigley Company Ltd

31st December 2017

Dear Javeen,

Thank you very much for your letter dated 14th December. It's always great to hear from you too! - even though you got my name wrong – it's Colin, not Simon!

One thing though – your letter is quite ambiguous. Are you saying (a) you've already got a Marketing Department so you don't need my assistance, or (b) you like my ideas so much you think I should apply to join your Marketing Department? Hopefully it's the latter. Certainly it seems you're currently missing a trick regarding body tattoo advertising.

Please can you clarify which one you meant. In the meantime, I will be pulling together my curriculum vitae, just in case you require it.

Kind regards,
Colin Montague, BSc (Hons), MSc

In the end, I wrote five more letters to companies about my tattoo sponsorship idea...

"To this end, I would like to propose that I get 12cm x 6cm tattoo on my left buttock that says "**Subway**" and a similar one on my right buttock that says "**Eat Fresh!**"

"...on my left buttock that says "**Yorkie**" and a similar one on my right buttock that says "**It's not for girls**"

"...on my left buttock that says "**Galaxy**" and a similar one on my right buttock that says "**Instant hot chocolate**"

"...on my left buttock that says "**Lindt**" and a similar one on my right buttock that says "**Master chocolatier**"

"...on my left buttock that says "**John Lewis**" and a similar one on my right buttock that says "**Never knowingly undersold**"

20th December 2017

Dear Mr. Montague,

Thank you very much for taking the time to contact us and for your interest in our products; we apologise for the delay with getting back to you.

Please note that we do not advertise our products using the body skin, therefore we are not interested in your offer.

Lindt & Sprüngli takes pride in manufacturing and marketing fine premium chocolate since more than 170 years. Our objective is to make available our delicate products to all kind of gourmets all over the world who appreciate our quality, our tradition, and our passion for chocolate. We respect diversity and high ethical values, regardless of gender, religion, political opinion or other convictions.

We hope for your understanding and thank you again for taking the time to contact us.

Yours sincerely,
Fiona W.

Lindt & Sprüngli

But only one more responded

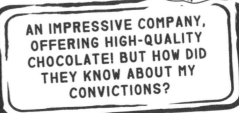

AN IMPRESSIVE COMPANY, OFFERING HIGH-QUALITY CHOCOLATE! BUT HOW DID THEY KNOW ABOUT MY CONVICTIONS?

I believe the Royal Family share my values and would appreciate what I've been doing.

Does the Honours and Appointments Secretariat in the Cabinet Office get many requests like this?

12th April 2017

Dear Sir/Madam,

My name is Colin Montague and I have now lived on Nutley Lane, Reigate for a number of years. We get a lot of young people walking down our lane, especially coming back from the pubs late at night. So over the years I have made it my business to quietly go around the road picking up litter (I once actually put a sign in our local notice board, asking for other volunteers, but nobody ever responded).

As a result of my tireless efforts, our beautiful little lane hasn't been spoilt by unsightly crisp packets, kebab wrappers and beer cans.

I believe the Royal Family share my values and would appreciate what I've been doing. I would therefore like to nominate myself for a knighthood (a smaller one, like MBE). Please can you send me the appropriate paperwork so I can get started on my application.

Kind regards,
Colin Montague, BSc (Hons), MSc

20th April 2017

Dear Mr. Montague,

Thank you for your letter of 12th April 2017 nominating yourself for an honour.

This will be disappointing for you but it not usual to recommend honours for anyone on the basis of a self nomination. However it is still possible for you to be considered. You need to arrange for someone else, who has direct knowledge of your voluntary/community work, to nominate you. You will also need to provide the minimum of two letters of support from people who know about your activities.

I have enclosed an honours nomination form which you should give to a colleague, friend or relative to complete on your behalf. The guidelines enclosed explain the procedures to follow.

Yours Sincerely
Jack H., Honours & Appointments Secretariat

Cabinet Office

To cut to the chase, I'm writing because I have a concern with which I would like some assistance

DELIGHTFUL!

OF ALL THE CURRENT PRIME MINISTERS SHE'S MY FAVOURITE!

TERRIFIC!

Is our Prime Minister, the Rt. Hon. Teresa May, willing to "help the little guy"?

20th February 2017

Dear Mrs. May,

Firstly may I say congratulations on becoming Prime Minister last year and I wish you all the very best in the role.

To cut to the chase, I'm writing because I have a concern with which I would like some assistance. My house has a single-car driveway in the front garden and the local council has clearly marked white lines outside our house to stop cars parking outside on the road. But we still get cars encroaching on the white lines, making it hard for me to get my car out. It's absolutely infuriating!

I know that you are busy at the moment, negotiating our country's exit from the European Community, but I would be most grateful if you could help in this matter – or at least advise where I should go to get some assistance.

Thank you very much in advance for any help you can provide.

Kind regards,
Colin Montague, BSc (Hons), MSc

23rd April 2017

Dear Mr. Montague,

I am writing on behalf of the Prime Minister to thank you for your letter of 20 February.

Mrs. May very much appreciates the time you have taken to write to her.

As the Department for Transport has responsibility for the matters you raise, I am forwarding your letter to them so that they are aware of your views.

Thank you, once again, for writing.

Yours sincerely,
R.D., Correspondence Officer

Prime Minister's Office, No. 10 Downing Street

I'm writing to organise our first social get-together

**The deputy manager of The Grantley Arms seems like a great guy.**

2nd December 2017

Dear Sir/Madam,

I am the Co-Chairman of a small online support group for people living in Surrey who suffer from mild paranoia. I'm writing to organise our first social get-together, and we are looking to have a dinner party at your restaurant in the New Year. We are very flexible on the dates (some time in January), but before we book, please can you let me know your hygiene rating. Also, do you have a private room or area we can use?

As soon as I get your response I hope to make a booking straight away.

Kind regards,
Colin Montague, BSc (Hons), MSc

10th December 2017

Dear Colin,

Thank you for your letter, requesting information for a dinner party in January. We are honoured that you have considered us for your first get together. We have been given the highest hygiene rating (5), which is something we are very proud of.

With regards to the area, we have a private room, which can host up to 22 people. Would this be suitable for you? And what would be your preferred date?

If it is easier, and quicker, our phone number is 01483 ******, or our email is info@thegrantleyarms.co.uk and we can get you booked in as soon as possible.

We look forward to your reply.

Kind regards
Ian G., Deputy Manager

The Grantley Arms

17th December 2017

Dear Ian,

Thanks very much for your kind response. There should be about 15 of us and our preferred date is Tuesday 23rd January. But I'm afraid some of the group members have asked me to find out a little more information before we make our booking: Firstly, please confirm our table will be served by only your most trusted and hygienic staff. Secondly, can you assure us there will be no cameras or recording devices near our table.

Sorry for this additional step. As soon as we get your response we will firm up the booking straight away.

Kind regards,
Colin Montague, BSc (Hons), MSc

Ps. Also, can I just ask you - the other day I received a few phone calls and nobody answered when I picked up. That wasn't you was it?

21st December 2017

Dear Colin,

Thank you for your reply. The 23rd January would be perfect, what time would you be looking for?

With regards to the cameras, we do not have CCTV so that wont be a problem at all, however I cannot guarantee that there won't be other customers with cameras (i.e. phones with cameras). Due to you being in our private room that shouldn't be a problem while you are seated at the table. We require all our staff to adhere to high levels on cleanliness and hygiene.

Kind regards
Ian G., Deputy Manager

The Grantley Arms

PS: I can confirm that it wasn't us who called you as we haven't been given a number yet. I hope you find out who it was.

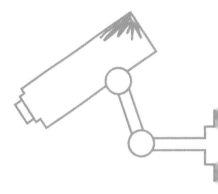

27th December 2017

Dear Ian,

Thanks for your latest response (you must be getting sick of dealing with me). I'm sorry to report that our group has had to cancel our inaugural dinner.

As you know, as Co-Chairman of our small online support group for people in Surrey suffering from mild paranoia, it was very clear to everyone that I was responsible for coordinating our group dinner. But Paul, the group's other Co-Chairman is constantly undermining my position and plotting to take over the task. I'M NOT GOING TO PUT UP WITH IT! So please cancel our reservation and if Paul calls you please do not believe anything he says about me - he's a LIAR.

Sorry to give you the bad news of our cancellation and "air our dirty laundry" in public like this. On a brighter side, my mild paranoia seems to be getting much better recently, so I'm thinking of leaving the group anyway.

Kind regards,
Colin Montague, BSc (Hons), MSc

Ps. Are you sure it wasn't you that called my phone?

Please confirm the rooms will allow smoking, include fully stocked minibars and have good quality soundproofing

Will the Ardington Hotel, along the Worthing Seafront welcome my anarcho-trash metal band?

17th December 2017

Dear Sir/Madam,

A dear friend of mine is the road manager of anarcho-trash metal band, Armia Chaosu (Army of Chaos), based out of Gdansk, Poland. They are touring the UK early next year and should be playing two nights in the Worthing area. I'm writing, as a favour to him, to see if five adjoining double rooms can be booked from Monday 5th to Wednesday 7th February.

I understand the band members usually like to bring a few select guests back to visit the rooms after the concerts for a quiet cocktail. Please confirm the rooms will allow smoking, include fully stocked minibars and have good quality soundproofing. Also, is hand-cream provided for free?

I await your positive response, at which time I will make the booking for my friend.

Kind regards,
Colin Montague,
BSc (Hons), MSC

23rd December 2017

Dear Mr. Montague,

Thank you for your kind enquiry regarding accommodation from Monday 5th to Wednesday 7th February 2018. Due to some of the points raised, my manager Richard would like to discuss this further over telephone or email if possible.

We close today (23rd December 2017) for the Christmas and New Year period and will reopen on January 8th 2018. We will be monitoring emails during this period so if you would like to send us an email with your telephone number, we will then call you promptly to discuss your kind enquiry further.

I look forward to hearing from you at your earliest convenience.

Best Wishes
Sophie, Reception

Ardington Hotel

REMARKABLE
VERY
UNDERSTANDING!
PEOPLE!

I know Disney goes out of its way to look after its guests

LONG LIVE MICKEY!
THE WORLD'S BEST PLACE TO GO ON HOLIDAY!!!
LONG LIVE MICKEY!

How could anyone possibly be concerned about visiting the wonderful Disneyland Paris?

20th February 2017

Dear Sir/Madam,

I'm planning a visit to your theme park with my wife in June this year, but before I book our tickets, I need your assistance with a rather embarrassing problem – I suffer from acute suriphobia (fear of anything to do with mice). As such, I have a concern that I'm going to accidentally come into close proximity with either Mickey or Minnie Mouse and that even being around the larger-than-life characters is going to trigger some sort of panic attack.

I don't want this to spoil my trip, but it's making me anxious just thinking about it. I know Disney goes out of its way to look after its guests, so please - if I tell you the dates of our visit, is there a way to ensure that I stay on the opposite sides of the park from where these two will be? Perhaps if I knew where they were going to be in advance, I could make sure I'm always somewhere else.

I look forward to hearing from you at your earliest convenience.

Kind regards,
Colin Montague,
BSc (Hons), MSc

STILL AWAITING A RESPONSE

I understand that I simply have to make a minimum £25 donation and your announcer will read out up to 50 words

---

Does the Brockham Bonfire Committee accept any sponsorship at all for its fireworks?

9th November 2017

Dear Madam,

I have attended your excellent annual Brockham Bonfire and Firework Display for the past five years and have noticed that you offer the opportunity to sponsor a firework with a small donation. So I have a slightly unusual request:

I am a strong supporter of North Korea's leader, Kim Jong-un. As such, I would like to sponsor a firework at next year's display in his honour. I understand that I simply have to make a minimum £25 donation and your announcer will read out up to 50 words.

My proposed wording would be: "And we have a firework in honour of the Dear Leader, Kim Jong-un, Exulted Leader of the Democratic People's Republic of Korea, Chairman of the Korean Workers' Party and Supreme Commander of the Korean People's Army. Our love, respect and best wishes from all your supporters in Reigate."

Please can you confirm that this would not be a problem.

Kind regards,
Colin Montague, BSc (Hons), MSc

AN OUTSTANDING FIREWORK DISPLAY! ONE OF THE BEST IN BRITAIN!

STILL AWAITING A RESPONSE

I'm actually writing on behalf of a dear friend of mine, who lives in the area and is simply too embarrassed to ask the question herself

AN INCREDIBLE LOCAL COUNCIL, DOING AN OUTSTANDING JOB!

STILL AWAITING A RESPONSE

What's Reigate & Banstead Council's advice on how best to dispose of Lulu?

26th January 2017

Dear Sir/Madam,

Firstly, let me say I'm personally very happy with the service I get from the council. In this instance, I'm actually writing on behalf of a dear friend of mine, who lives in the area and is simply too embarrassed to ask the question herself.

It's quite a delicate matter. She's had a pet tortoise, Lulu, for the past 37 years, but she's concerned that one day in the near future she will inevitably pass from this realm (Lulu, not my friend). Lulu is her first and only pet, and having never been in this position before, she's not sure she knows the right etiquette for what one is supposed to do with disposing of a fairly large tortoise cadaver.

Could you please advise if there is a way for the council to dispose of the remains. If so, do you do something formal such as a religious service (I would say Lulu would probably be C of E), or is it just a case of putting her out with the bins on Thursday? If so, and I'm sorry to have to ask this, would she go in the brown bin (I suppose technically she's biodegradable), or should she just use the regular green bin? I'm presuming it's not the black bin, since as far as I know she is not recyclable.

Any advice you can provide would be gratefully received.

Kind regards,
Colin Montague, BSc (Hons), MSc

I think your shops bring real value to consumers

I'm happy to report that this rumour about Poundland turned out to be wrong...

20th February 2017

Dear Sir/Madam,

Firstly, let me say that I have been a loyal customer of several branches of Poundland for many years. I think your shops bring real value to consumers - especially the less affluent.

I am writing to ask you to address a concern I have. Last night in the local pub I was told by several friends who I trust that, due to the cumulative affect of years of albeit relatively low inflation, Poundland is now considering rebranding itself as the "£1.02 Store" later in the year. This is alarming.

I think this is a serious mistake and would greatly undermine the trust that Poundland has built up in its customer base over the years. Please can you confirm whether or not this rumour is true. If it is the case, then I would strongly urge you to rethink.

Best regards,
Colin Montague, BSc (Hons), MSc

A STUPENDOUS STORE, OFFERING GREAT CUSTOMER VALUE!

STILL AWAITING A RESPONSE

My wife and I are quite new to the "scene", but we are always willing to try something new!

Are B&D Plastics Ltd. still contemplating my alternative use for its products?

12th March 2017

Dear Sir/Madam,

My wife and I are quite new to the "scene", but we are always willing to try something new! We recently heard about your company through an acquaintance and it's made us curious. In brief, we've tried leather, lace, vinyl, rubber and latex - but never plastic. How does it feel on the skin? Please could you send us a catalogue of your products.

Thank you for your assistance and we look forward to hearing from you in the near future.

Best regards,
Colin Montague, BSc (Hons), MSc

STILL
AWAITING
RESPONSES

We were particularly excited by the idea of your "S&M Positive Injection Pump"

S&M Electronics sounds like it offers some exciting products!

12th March 2017

Dear Sir/Madam,

My wife and I have only really been into "the scene" for the past two years, but when we recently overheard a conversation about your products we felt we had to look you up and get in contact.
We were particularly excited by the idea of your "S&M Positive Injection Pump". Please could you tell us how it works, how much it costs and also, is it unisex?

Thank you for your assistance in this matter.

Your obedient servant,
Colin Montague, BSc (Hons), MSc

Chapter Three:
Important Questions

Whevever I have a nagging question in my head I just ask it. I find it makes life so much simpler! Once people get over their initial bemusement, they're usually more than happy to give me an answer....

I'm writing so far in advance because we have a rather delicate issue, requiring a bit of advanced planning...

Is the famous Alton Towers theme park happy to respond to my unusual question?

4th February 2017

Dear Sir/Madam,

My wife and I are very excited to be planning a visit to your theme park, probably sometime in late July – especially as we rarely get out much these days. I'm writing so far in advance because we have a rather delicate issue, requiring a bit of advanced planning:

My wife weighs 600 lbs, so is quite a large lady. Regarding the fun park, I just need to check which rides she will be able to access. Please could you also confirm that the water park will not be a problem.

I look forward to hearing from you at your earliest convenience.

Kind regards,
Colin Montague, BSc (Hons), MSc

Ps. We actually drive a small/medium-sized flatbed truck – would we still be able to park it in the regular parking area?

15th February 2017

Dear Colin,

Thank you for taking the time to write to the Alton Towers Resort regarding your upcoming visit.

The Rides at the Alton Towers Resort operate with restrictive harnesses in order to keep our guests safe and secure at all times. After discussing your query with the rides team we have concluded that we don't believe that are rides would be suitable or comfortable for your wife to ride.
We do have alternative attractions at the Theme Park including Sharkbait Reef by Sea Life Centre and our historic gardens.

The Waterpark will be fine, however again we don't feel the attractions or the slides will be suitable.

Regarding your question about parking your flatbed truck, will depend on its length and width, we may be able to organise a space in our bus park if that is something that would prefer.

If you have any further questions please don't hesitate to get in touch.

Kind Regards
Matt, Customer Services

Alton Towers Resort

SPECTACULAR PLACE - & A SUPER-FUN DAY OUT!

I am certain there must be others like me who are equally perplexed by this ambiguous system...

Can the Compass Travel bus company explain to me how the bus system works?

20th November 2017

Dear Sir/Madam,

I do not normally take buses, but last week my daughter's car was in for a service and I took the No.32 bus from Reigate to Dorking by myself. But when I wanted to go home, it took me a while to realise that I had to take a bus with *the same number* back to Reigate!

This is very confusing. Surely if the bus is going in the opposite direction it should have a different number? I am certain there must be others like me who are equally perplexed by this ambiguous system. I strongly suggest you consider changing your numbering system and would very much appreciate your feedback on this idea.

King regards,
Colin Montague, BSc (Hons), MSc

22nd November 2017

Dear Mr. Montague,

Thank you for your letter of 20th November, the contents of which I was a bit confused to read. All buses up and down the country run the same service number both ways on each individual route. If we were to give each direction on each route a different number, then this would cause an awful lot of confusion up and down the country. Every bus company runs the same system so as not to cause any confusion in the industry to our passengers.

I hope this clarifies the situation for you.

Yours sincerely,
Amanda B.

Compass Travel (Sussex) Limited

SENSIBLE PEOPLE
PERFORMING AN INVALUABLE SERVICE! & THANKS SO MUCH FOR EXPLAINING HOW IT WORKS!
SENSIBLE PEOPLE

He is particularly worried about improving his diet, reducing his intake of red meat, fried food, and saturated fats...

Will Heinz Group help me with a question about my Dad?

17th October 2017

Dear Sir/Madam,

My elderly father recently underwent an operation to insert a stent into one of his coronary arteries. Thankfully, he is recovering well, but still adjusting to life after the operation. Aside from wanting to commence some mild exercise, he is particularly worried about improving his diet, reducing his intake of red meat, fried food, and saturated fats. Would I be right in telling him that your baked beans are a good source of nutrients and can form part of a healthy balanced diet for his recovery?

I look forward to receiving your response at your earliest convenience.

Kind regards,
Colin Montague, BSc (Hons), MSc

23rd October 2017

Dear Mr. Montague,

Thank you for getting in touch with us.

Our five a day labelling is a helpful reminder of the contribution Heinz varieties can play in a healthy diet. Our soups, beans and spaghetti on which they appear are low in fat and sugar, and have also benefited from salt reduction in line with the Department of Health's Responsibility Deal targets. All our labelling is based on the 80g fruit and veg portion. For Spaghetti in Tomato Sauce of course this comes from the tomatoes.

A 200g serving of Heinz Beans contains one of your five-a-day target intake of fruit and vegetables. The portion comes from the beans themselves, which can only be counted once in any single day.

We hope the above information is helpful.

Yours sincerely,
Christine B., Consumer Care Co-Ordinator

H.J. Heinz Foods UK Ltd.

5th November 2017

Dear Christine,

Thank you for your letter dated 23rd October. It was very helpful. Based on what you said, I gave my father the very encouraging news that baked beans are good for his heart, but did warn him that "the more you eat the more you fart". However, on the positive side, the more you fart the better you feel - so I suggested he should eat them with his daily meal.

He's been taking my advice and feeling much healthier now. Thank you once again.

Kind regards,
Colin Montague, BSc (Hons), MSc

I acquired an emotional support animal (a miniature pig called Derek) and as a consequence have recently become a vegetarian

---

Tea Pigs make great tea – but I have a question for them...

12th April 2017

Dear Sir/Madam,

I have heard great things about your tea through a friend of mine who very much enjoys it. I'm quite embarrassed to ask this, but I have a quick question.

Earlier this year I acquired an emotional support animal (a miniature pig called Derek) and as a consequence of his friendship have recently become a vegetarian. So my question is this - your company's name is a little confusing; please can you confirm that all your varieties of tea are entirely vegetarian (or at least let me know which ones are).

I look forward to hearing a positive response from you at your earliest convenience, at which time I can hopefully start enjoying some of your teas.

Kind regards,
Colin Montague, BSc (Hons), MSc

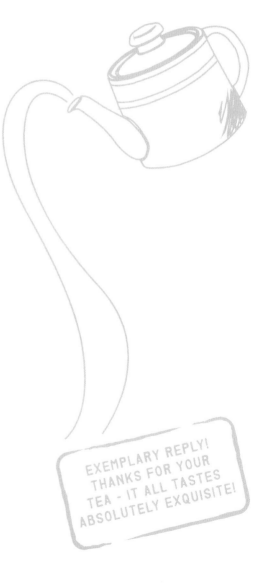

EXEMPLARY REPLY!
THANKS FOR YOUR
TEA - IT ALL TASTES
ABSOLUTELY EXQUISITE!

Hi Colin,

Thanks so much for writing to us! Derek sounds like a lovely chap who we'd all get on with just fine!

Rest assured that all of our teas are indeed vegetarian (although not all are vegan), and more info can be found on individual product pages on our website.

Please enjoy these samples as a starter pack!

Happy brewing! Leonie i

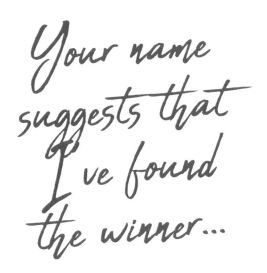

Your name suggests that I've found the winner...

Will a take-away business called "Perfect Kebab" provide hard evidence to support its name?

17th October 2017

Dear Sir,

My choir will be visiting your area on the evening of Saturday 11th November and I know we will want to eat in the very finest kebab shop that Carshalton has to offer. We all absolutely love kebabs.

Your name suggests that I've found the winner - but I've also found a place called Supa Kebab in Carshalton and another called Perfect Kebab in nearby Wallington.

So which is the real No.1? "Best", "Supa", or "Perfect"? I'm so confused. Please can you write to me and explain, so we can plan our night in advance.

Kind regards,
Colin Montague, BSc (Hons), MSc

27th October 2017

Dear Sir,

At Perfect Kebab, we want to thank you for writing to us and having us as an option for your night out in Wallington. We have been in Wallington for more than 11 years and we have always kept the Quality of our kebabs we serve to the best.

All our kebabs are prepared in our premises and all our Lamb kebabs are 100% Lamb. We are the only place that makes its own Lamb Doner kebab in Wallington, so that's what makes a big difference between us and other kebab shops.

Perfect Kebab would love to have your custom for your night out and anymore visits you are looking to make in Wallington. As a promise from us you will not be disappointed of your visit. We are looking forward to seeing you.

Kind Regards,
Perfect kebab

THESE ARE GOOD PEOPLE. PLEASE TAKE THE TIME TO VISIT THIS PLACE - AND TELL THEM COLIN SENT YOU!

I am writing with a small concern regarding your slogan...

Has Compare the Market noticed this simple mistake?

14th November 2017

Dear Sir/Madam,

Firstly, let me say thank you for providing a great service on your website. I have found it very useful in the past. But I am writing with a small concern regarding your slogan "Simples". There is no "s"; it should surely just be "Simple". Also, given that the UK is exiting Europe, wouldn't it be an appropriate time to find a meerkat with an *English* accent?

I'm sorry to be so pedantic, but I would be most grateful if you could respond with your thoughts.

Kind regards,
Colin Montague, BSc (Hons), MSc

Dear Mr. Colin Montague,

We have received your letter and I would like to thank you for taking the time to write into us. We appreciate your feedback and we will ensure that this gets passed on to the relevant team.

If there is anything else we can help you with, please do get back in touch. You can do this by emailing us, or visiting our Social Media channels.

Kind regards,
Aisling, Customer Support Team

comparethemarket.com

I LOVE THESE PEOPLE

SENSATIONALS
CUSTOMER
SUPPORT

INCOMPARABLE

I noticed that you have stopped using the slogan

I grew up with Kelloggs Frosties, so I do actually believe they're gr-r-reat!

14th November 2017

Dear Sir/Madam,

I recently bought a box of Kelloggs Frosties for the first time in many years and I have to say that I really enjoyed them. It reminded me of my childhood. But I noticed that you have stopped using the slogan "They're gr-r-reat!" I was wondering why that was. Is it because of the spelling mistake? I certainly think it's a shame that it's gone.

Will you be bringing it back at any point in the future perhaps with the correct spelling?

Kind regards,
Colin Montague, BSc (Hons), MSc

17th November 2017

Dear Mr. Montague,

Thacks for setting us know that you enjoy our Kellogg's® Frosties. I'm absolutely delighted to get such positive feedback, that's what we like to hear.

We're glad to hear that you think They're Gr-r-reat! We'll be sure to pass your comments on to our marketing team.

As a thank you I would like to send you a voucher towards your next purchase to help you buy some more of your favourite or try one of our other foods.

Thanks again for taking the time to get in touch - I hope you'll continue to enjoy our products for many years to come.

Yours sincerely,
Matthew S., Consumer Affairs Representative

Kellogg Marketing & Sales Company (UK) Limited

AN OUTSTANDING RESPONSE! & ALWAYS MY FIRST CHOICE FOR A BREAKFAST CEREAL

I don't know if you get asked this question very often

Have many people asked the candle company, La Montana, the same question?

17th December 2017

Dear Jonathan,

Firstly, let me say we absolutely love burning candles. In fact, my wife and I usually have about ten on the go in our living room most evenings. We like the look of your website, so we're writing to see if you can help us with a dilemma:

In anticipation of the warmer months approaching again, we recall previous summers where the heat from all our candles just made the hot nights unbearable. I don't know if you get asked this question very often, but if different substances burn at different temperatures, do you manufacture a candle that burns at a substantially lower temperature than most others?

Obviously luke-warm would be ideal, but I don't know if that's possible. Please can you let us know at your earliest convenience, because if you did, we would be extremely interested in buying a large quantity.

Kind regards,
Colin Montague, BSc (Hons), MSc

21st December 2017

Dear Colin,

Thank you very much for your letter. I'll try to answer it as well as I can but, in truth, I'm no expert on this specific topic. In fact, it's been something of an education finding out about it.

The first thing to mention is that our candles are made of mineral wax. When it comes to scented candles, mineral wax is universally regarded as giving the best scent 'throw'. both hot and cold - and we're all about the fragrance. Mineral wax has a melting point that's somewhere in the middle as far as candle waxes are concerned: soy wax melts at 54C, mineral wax at 57C and beeswax at 63C. A higher melting point wax produces less 'soot' and better scent throw, but burns faster. So mineral wax is the best compromise.

However... as far as your specific question goes, it seems that - despite varying melting points - the actual flames of candles, and therefore the heat they give out, are more or less the same. So, in short, I think it's more about the number of candles (or wicks) you have burning than the type of wax.

The only thing I can recommend is a reed diffuser or two, just to reduce the number of open flames.

Hope that helps.

Have a very happy Christmas.

All the best
Jonathan H.
La Montana

I am concerned that the deplorable practice of child marriage has come to Reigate

---

Am I unearthing the shocking truth about child brides in Surrey?

17th December 2017

Dear Sir/Madam,

Would you mind telling me the intended age range for the small bride outfit currently in your shop window? I am concerned that the deplorable practice of child marriage has come to Reigate, so any reassurance that you can give me that this isn't the case would be appreciated.

Kind regards,
Colin Montague, BSc (Hons), MSc

STILL AWAITING A RESPONSE

I understand that you can rent out a screening room to show the film of your choice

I didn't get exactly what I wanted from Oxted Cinema – but it wasn't a cat-astrophe!

18th March 2018

Dear Sir/Madam,

I was fortunate enough to visit your beautiful cinema a few months ago, since the major renovation and I very much enjoyed the experience - very comfy chairs and great snacks! Furthermore, I understand that one can rent out a screening room to show the film of one's choice at a very reasonable rate.

So I would like to ask you a question on behalf of my friend, Antonia. She lives for her cats and her eldest cat, Marmalade, will be celebrating his 17th birthday in May. To mark this special occasion, please would it be possible to rent out a smaller screening room to show The Aristocats movie, as this has always been a firm favourite of Marmalade's.

It would just be Antonia, Marmalade, perhaps 4-5 select friends in attendance, as well as Antonia's 35 other cats. Please could you let me know whether it would be convenient for the morning of Monday 21st May and how much this would cost.

Kind regards,
Colin Montague, BSc (Hons), MSc

Dear Colin,

Thank you very much for your letter. We appreciate your interest in our cinema and we're happy you enjoy the experience we offer.

Marmalade's birthday party sounds like a great idea, I love The Aristocats movie as well. However amazing this sounds we are unable to host this event. Currently we do not offer private hires for pets.

We're sending you some complimentary tickets as thanks for the interest and sorry that we cannot help.

Thank you very much for you interest, please do not hesitate to get in touch with any further queries.

Warmest regards,
Dominika D., Private Hire

Everyman

THAT'S AN EXTRAORDINARY EXAMPLE OF CUSTOMER CARE!

I've been wearing my hair conservatively short at the front and sides, but quite a bit longer at the back

I'm sure PricewaterhouseCoopers genuinely values diversity in the workplace.

7th October 2018

Dear Sir/Madam,

I am writing because I am interested in a career within PricewaterhouseCoopers, but I first need some information regarding your equal opportunity employment practices, in order for me to feel comfortable applying for a job.

I've been wearing my hair conservatively short at the front and sides, but quite a bit longer at the back. This means I come up against a surprising amount of prejudice in my daily life. Haters often call me terms such as a "mullet head", "neckwarmer", "80/20", or other similar epithets - all of which I find quite offensive.

Please can you assure me that my hairstyle will not be held against me when considering my candidacy for a job.

Kind regards,
Colin Montague, BSc (Hons), MSc

PWC IS STILL MY IDEA OF A PERFECT COMPANY!

STILL AWAITING A RESPONSE

My life always seems to be far more hectic than I'd like...

Tag Heuer make amazing watches – but it's about time they responded to my letter.

12th April 2018

Dear Sir/Madam,

I'm writing to ask you earnestly for your advice. Years ago when I was a lot younger, I used to own a watch that was a particular favourite of mine, because it always ran a little slow. Then one day it just stopped. But back then I always seemed to have so much more time to get things done. I attribute this to that watch.

Now I've owned a TAG Aquaracer for the past three years (a beautiful-looking watch by the way) it always seems to keep impeccable timing - and that is my problem. As a consequence, my life always seems to be far more hectic than I'd like. I attribute this in some measure to my watch.

I imagine you must get this request quite often - please could you recommend me a watch that runs a little slower so I can get my life back to a more acceptable pace.

I would greatly appreciate any assistance you can provide.

Kind regards,
Colin Montague, BSc (Hons), MSc

I SUPPOSE I'LL JUST STICK WITH MY BEAUTIFUL AND VERY ACCURATE TAG AQUARACER!

STILL AWAITING A RESPONSE

I've recently been looking at the moon...

Has the Royal Astronomical Society noticed the same thing I have?

9th November 2017

Dear Madam,

I have recently been looking at the moon and it looks a lot nearer than it used to be when I was younger. I am very worried about this, because if it keeps this up it will probably hit us. Am I the only to have noticed this? Also, is it going to eventually hit or miss Earth and are we going to be safe?

I hope to hear from you soon, and I sincerely hope that you can put my mind at rest.

Kind regards,
Colin Montague, BSc (Hons), MSc

IN MY HUMBLE OPINION, THESE GUYS ARE THE BEST ASTRONOMICAL SOCIETY IN THE WHOLE OF CENTRAL LONDON!

STILL AWAITING A RESPONSE

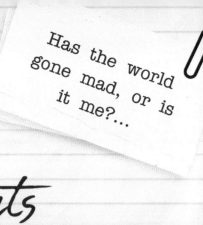

Has the world gone mad, or is it me?...

Chapter Four:
Mild Complaints

I have always been a loyal customer of Burger King

Can Burger King, one of the UK's favourite burger chains, solve a mystery?

5th February 2017

Dear Sir/Madam,

I have always been a loyal customer of Burger King, but I am writing to express my concern and distaste at some of your company's recent marketing material: While on a recent trip to the South of Wales I was walking through a local market when I came across several varieties of men's undergarments (both briefs and boxers), emblazoned across the front with a picture of a hamburger and just above it, your famous slogan "Home of the Whopper".

I really don't think that this rude euphemism is an appropriate way to market your product and I am alarmed that your company evidently takes a different view on this. I had always believed Burger King stood for great tasting food and good clean family fun. So I would very much like to understand the thinking behind why you are doing this and I would like your reassurance that you won't be adopting the same advertising campaign in England.

Kind regards,
Colin Montague, BSc (Hons), MSc

1st March 2017

Dear Mr. Montague,

Thank you for taking the time to contact BURGER KING® Guest Relations regarding our current advertising. As a valued guest, your feedback is very important to us.

Thank you again for bringing this matter to our attention and rest assured that your comments have been forwarded to the appropriate management team so that they may be aware of your concerns.

We value your opinion and look forward to serving you again in the near future.

Kind Regards,
Guest Relations

BURGER KING®

IN RETROSPECT, I THINK I MIGHT HAVE BEEN A LITTLE CONFUSED. BUT WHAT'S CERTAIN IS THAT BK ALWAYS SERVES ME SUPREMELY TASTY FOOD!

Admittedly I am probably a little over-sensitive, having recently struck up a strong bond with a miniature pig...

Bocketts Farm is a favourite local venue for a family day out - but am I right to have a concern?

21st April 2017

Dear Sir/Madam,

I'm writing to express a concern: Friends of mine recently told me they took their young daughter to your farm and, amongst a host of fun activities, they actually watched pig racing. I didn't get all the details and I don't profess to know much about it, but I am genuinely worried for the safety and well-being of the pigs. I don't think they're meant to have people put saddles on them and ride them - certainly not competitively. And I'm sure it's not good for their backs.

Admittedly I am probably a little over-sensitive, having recently struck up a strong bond with a miniature pig (his name is Derek). But I would sincerely appreciate anything you could say to allay my concerns regarding the welfare of these beautiful creatures.

Kind regards,
Colin Montague, BSc (Hons), MSc
A pig-lover

Dear Colin,

Thank you for your recent letter.

I am sorry to hear that you are so concerned about our pig races and pigs. I'd like to assure you that the welfare of our animals is paramount and that they are all very loved and well looked after.

I agree that pigs should never be ridden and we wouldn't dream of allowing people to ride them, competitively or not. Our pigs run around a short track to eat their lunch and then are left to play in the paddock at the end. Nothing is put on their backs at all and it is clear to see that they all enjoy it.

Please do not hesitate to get in touch should you wish to discuss the matter further.

Yours sincerely,
Hannah G., General Manager

Bocketts Farm

FLAWLESS

SUCH A FUN PLACE TO VISIT FOR THE WHOLE FAMILY!

RESPONSE

I bought a loaf of Hovis bread and I genuinely thought it tasted delicious...

In retrospect I think my expectations of Hovis might've been a little unrealistic.

28th September 2017

Dear Sir/Madam,

I'm writing to complain about misleading advertising on your product: A while ago I bought a loaf of Hovis bread and I genuinely thought it tasted delicious. Then I went away on an extended holiday for six months, came back home, went to make a sandwich and - there was some mould on my bread. Yet I've always understood that this shouldn't happen, from your advertising catch phrase "Hovis, as good today as it's always been" - certainly not this particular loaf!

I should be most grateful if you could either refund the £1.06 or explain where I've gone wrong in my understanding.

Kind regards,
Colin Montague, BSc (Hons), MSc

9th October 2017

Dear Mr. Montague,

Thank you for your letter dated 28th September 2017 regarding our advertising on our Hovis products.

Our advertising caption "Hovis, as good today as it's always been" is a reference to the quality of baking over the last 130 years and that we still produce the same great quality.

At Hovis we pride ourselves in our bread making but unfortunately we cannot guarantee to keep the freshness and taste after the best before date.

Once again thank you for taking the time to write to us.

Yours sincerely,
Carol W., Customer Service Advisor

Hovis

OH MY GOODNESS
TO ME THIS IS THE BEST BREAD IN THE WORLD!
VERY HELPFUL STAFF TOO!

My favourite is the Aromatic Lamb Curry with Rice and Lentil Pilaf

---

Can Marks & Spencer give me any practical feedback for my problem?

12th April 2017

Dear Sir/Madam,

I have been trying to lose weight for a long time and a friend of mine recently put me onto your BALANCED FOR YOU range, as she said it had worked well for her (my favourite is the Aromatic Lamb Curry with Rice and Lentil Pilaf).

She said if I ate these meals more often I would start to lose weight. But I've been eating them pretty much solidly now for the past three weeks and to my alarm I haven't lost any weight at all - in fact I've gained two pounds!

I've got up to about eight a day and it's costing me a small fortune. This is ridiculous. Please can you advise at what point people usually start losing weight. Do I need to increase to ten a day? I'm extremely frustrated by the whole thing, so any help would be gratefully appreciated.

Thank you and kind regards,
Colin Montague, BSc (Hons), MSc

UNPARALLELED EMPATHETIC, KIND AND HELPFUL! SERVICE!

21st April 2017

Dear Mr. Montague,

I'm sorry to hear about the problems you've had when trying to lose weight, I think this is something we can all relate to! We don't sell our Balanced for you range as a weight loss range but more of a way to help you be more healthier as they are lower calorie dishes. We do have a nutrition website that has lots of information about getting healthier and also tips on how to loose weight. I hope this information has been helpful. Thank you for getting in touch.

Yours sincerely
Alicia H., Retail Customer Services

Marks and Spencer plc

I thought at first it was just a one-off, but then I took a second bite.

I wrote to Nestlé to complain about their delicious Aero bars – but my argument is full of holes.

28th September 2017

Dear Sir/Madam,

I'm writing to express a concern regarding your Aero bars and more specifically to ask for a partial refund. I bought an Aero today, I think for around £1.00 at a local store, bit into it and was alarmed to discover that it was full of holes! I thought at first it was just a one-off, but then I took a second bite and found more holes!

Please can you send me a refund for at least 30 pence to allow for the holes.

Kind regards,
Colin Montague, BSc (Hons), MSc

3rd October 2017

Hello Colin,

Thank you for your recent letter.

We were sorry to hear of your disappointment with Aero Bar.

We believe in producing products with a great taste, consistent levels of quality and safety, value for money and convenience. We are very sorry that you have not enjoyed your Aero Bar this time.

Aero was introduced in 1935. In 1959 Peppermint was added to the range along with Orange in 1985. It is a classic deliciously light bubbles encased in smooth chocolate.

We have not made any recent changes to this product. However we value your comments and will pass your feedback to the brand team. Perhaps I could suggest trying our Yorkie Bars which are solid chocolate.

Finally, thank you for taking the time and trouble to advise us of your dissatisfaction. Contact with our consumers provides an invaluable contribution in protecting and improving the standard of our products and services.

Yours sincerely
Sue T., Contact Centre Executive
Consumer Engagement Services

Nestlé UK Ltd

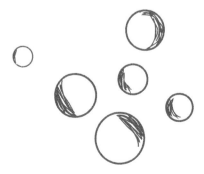

IT TURNS OUT I WAS WRONG – APPARENTLY AEROS HAVE ALWAYS HAD HOLES. I'VE NOW STARTED EATING THEM QUITE A LOT, BECAUSE THEY TASTE SO GOOD!

Something has recently come to my attention and I feel I must write

MY MISTAKE - I APOLOGISE! IT TURNS OUT THEY'RE JUST EASY-TO-MAKE, DELICIOUS-TASTING MEALS!

Unilever make delicious Pot Noodle – but have I misunderstood something about this snack?

12th April 2017

Dear Sir/Madam,

Something has recently come to my attention and I feel I must write: I understand that you are selling a product called "Pot Noodle".

While I appreciate you are a Dutch company and marijuana, or "pot" as you like to call it, is legal there, I am very unhappy at the thought of you peddling such a product in the U.K. – I am particularly worried about the potential damage to our younger generation.

So I would appreciate a response as to why your company feels this is acceptable behaviour. I just don't understand it.

Kind regards,
Colin Montague, BSc (Hons), MSc

STILL AWAITING A RESPONSE

If you think I over-complicate my life in Reigate, you should see some of the bad decisions I make when I go on holiday to relax

"Dear Sir/Madam, I'm writing to tell you about my recent stay at your hotel. There's no way to sugar-coat this - quite frankly, I was disappointed..."

I would very much like to thank Cassia Friello and Gary Standing for their wonderful artwork, which I think really brought the book to life. I'm also extremely grateful to my good friend Roland Moore for his endless patience and sound advice. Finally, I definitely need to thank all the companies I wrote to and particularly all the kind and generous-spirited employees who had to read all my nonsense and yet still took the time to give earnest and well-intentioned replies.

"Thank you for contacting us outlining the opportunity to sponsor your tattoo..."

"Thank you for the letter of 27th January concerning your 25th wedding anniversary celebration and your rather delicate matter..."

"Thank you for taking the time to write to us here at Caffè Nero regarding your idea of edible coffee cups..."

"I am writing on behalf of the Prime Minister to thank you for your letter of 20 February..."

"Thank you for your generous offer to donate your work *Quit While You're Ahead* to Tate Modern..."

35921249R00044

Printed in Great Britain
by Amazon